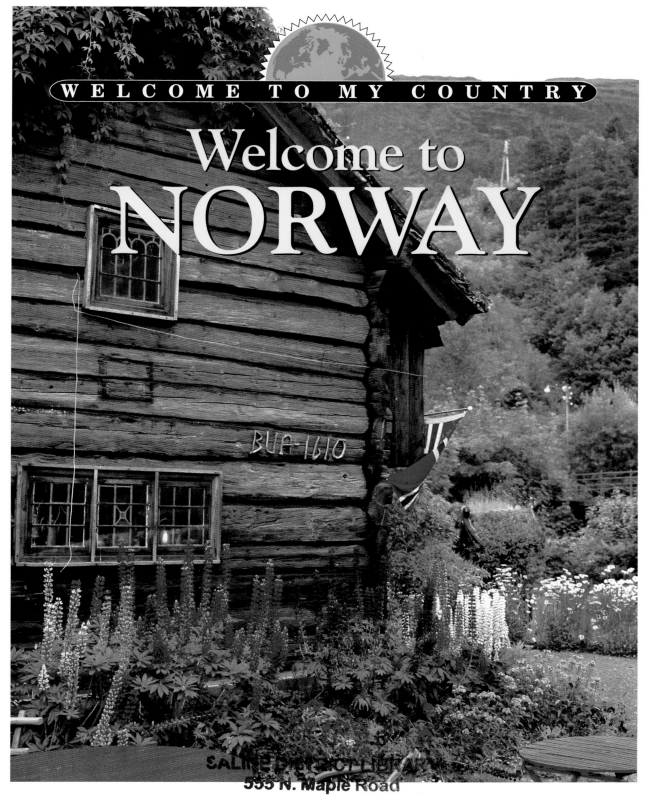

WELCOME TO MY COUNTRY

Welcome to
NORWAY

BUA-1610

Gareth Stevens Publishing
A WORLD ALMANAC EDUCATION GROUP COMPANY

Written by
VANESSA WAN

Edited by
MELVIN NEO

Edited in USA by
JOANN EARLY MACKEN

Designed by
GEOSLYN LIM

Picture research by
SUSAN JANE MANUEL

First published in North America in 2004 by
Gareth Stevens Publishing
A World Almanac Education Group Company
330 West Olive Street, Suite 100
Milwaukee, Wisconsin 53212 USA

Please visit our web site at:
www.garethstevens.com
For a free color catalog describing
Gareth Stevens Publishing's list of high-quality
books and multimedia programs,
call 1-800-542-2595 (USA) or
1-800-387-3178 (Canada).
Gareth Stevens Publishing's fax: (414) 332-3567.

© **TIMES MEDIA PRIVATE LIMITED 2004**
Originated and designed by
Times Editions
An imprint of Times Media Private Limited
A member of the Times Publishing Group
Times Centre, 1 New Industrial Road
Singapore 536196
http://www.timesone.com.sg/te

Library of Congress Cataloging-in-Publication Data
Wan, Vanessa.
Welcome to Norway / by Vanessa Wan.
p. cm. — (Welcome to my country)
Contents: Welcome to Norway! — The land — History —
Government and the economy — People and lifestyle —
Language — Arts — Leisure — Food.
Includes bibliographical references and index.
ISBN 0-8368-2562-4 (lib. bdg.)
1. Norway—Juvenile literature. [1. Norway.]
I. Title. II. Series.
DL409W36   2004
948.1—dc22   2003060162

Printed in Singapore

1 2 3 4 5 6 7 8 9 08 07 06 05 04

PICTURE CREDITS
Ellen Barone/Houserstock, Inc: 20, 41
Johan Berge: 23 (top)
Jan Butchofsky/Houserstock, Inc: 18
Dave G. Houser/Houserstock, Inc: 30,
    32, 33 (bottom), 37
Focus Team — Italy: 3, 8, 23 (bottom), 45
Getty Images/Hulton Archive: 11 (top),
    12, 13, 14, 15 (top), 29 (right)
Haga Library, Japan: cover, 3 (bottom),
    21, 33 (top), 35, 38 (both)
HBL Network Photo Agency: 2, 5, 6, 31, 34
Hutchison Library: 16
International Photobank: 1, 4, 43
Lonely Planet: 40 (both)
North Wind Picture Archives: 10
Scanpix/Norway: 15 (bottom), 17, 24, 28,
    29 (left), 39
David Simson: 19
Sylvia Cordaiy Photo Library: 7, 9, 22, 26
Topham Picturepoint: 11 (bottom), 25, 27 (both)

Digital Scanning by Superskill Graphics Pte Ltd

Contents

Words that appear in the glossary are printed in **boldface** type the first time they occur in the text.

Welcome to Norway!

The Kingdom of Norway is one of Europe's most mountainous countries. It is famous for its **trolls**, **fjords**, and Viking history. About 4.5 million people live in Norway, and the country enjoys one of the highest standards of living in Europe. Let's learn more about Norway and its people.

Opposite: Because two-thirds of Norway is covered with mountains, **glaciers** such as this are a common sight in the country.

Below: Norwegians are interested in nature. They have built cabins beside many fjords to be closer to the great outdoors.

The Flag of Norway

Norway's flag has a blue cross with a white outline set against a red background. Norway was part of a union with Denmark and later with Sweden. The Norwegian flag was first officially flown on December 15, 1899.

The Land

Norway has an area of 118,834 square miles (307,860 square kilometers), including many islands off its coast. To the east, Norway shares a border with Sweden, Finland, and Russia. Along the coast, it is surrounded by the Norwegian Sea, the North Atlantic Ocean, and the North Sea. Norway also has several glaciers, the largest of which is called Jostedalsbreen.

Below: Many fjords line the Norwegian coastline. The country's longest and deepest fjord is Sogne Fjord.

Norway is divided into four regions separated by mountain ranges: Nord-Norge in the north, Østlandet in the east, Trøndelag in the center, and Vestlandet in the west. The highest point in Norway is Galdhöpiggen, which rises to 8,100 feet (2,469 meters).

Oslo, the capital of Norway, is located in Østlandet, the most populated part of the country. The Glåma is Norway's longest river at 372 miles (599 km). The river generates **hydroelectric power** and is used to transport timber.

Above: Norway's first capital, known as Trøndheim, was founded in Sør-Trøndelag province in A.D. 997.

7

Seasons and the Climate

Although it is far to the north, Norway has a pleasant climate. Most parts of the country have snowy winters. The western coast, however, has milder weather because of the warm **Gulf Stream**. Average temperatures in Oslo are 25° Fahrenheit (−4° Celsius) in winter and 61° F (16° C) in summer. Norway is also called "The Land of the Midnight Sun" because areas in the north experience long hours of sunlight from mid-May through July.

Above: In the higher altitudes, there are many glaciers, but Norway's fjords and harbors are nearly ice free all year because the Gulf Stream brings in warm water.

Plants and Animals

Forests cover more than one-third of Norway. The most famous trees, the Norway spruce and the Scotch pine, are often used as Christmas trees.

Norway's wildlife includes elks, red deer, bears, wolves, and arctic animals such as reindeer. Its many varieties of birds include cranes, arctic terns, and cuckoos. Salmon and trout live in the lakes and rivers.

Below: In the Norwegian countryside, **domesticated** animals such as goats are a common sight.

History

The first **inhabitants** of Norway were probably hunters and fishermen. Later settlers farmed and raised livestock. The Vikings, who were fierce warriors, took over from A.D. 800 to A.D. 1100.

Early History

After many battles, Viking chief Harald I Fairhair began to unite Norway under his rule in the ninth century. In the eleventh century, his **descendant**, Olaf II Haraldsson, became king of Norway.

Below: The Vikings were **aggressive** fighters who were among the most feared warriors of their time.

Between 1349 and 1350, two-thirds of Norway's population died from a **plague** called the Black Death. The country's wealth and power declined. In 1380, King Olaf of Denmark united Norway and Denmark. By 1397, Denmark, Sweden, and Norway had joined to form the Kalmar Union. The Danish ruled Norway for the next four hundred years. In 1814, Norway became independent for a short time, but Sweden attacked and defeated it.

Above: The Black Death affected many countries in Europe during the fourteenth century.

Below: King Oscar II ruled both Sweden and Norway until 1905.

The Norwegian Throne

In 1884, a parliamentary government replaced the Swedish monarchy. In 1905, Norway's union with Sweden ended, and the Norwegian government elected Denmark's Prince Carl as king. Prince Carl took the name King Haakon VII.

Two World Wars

From 1905 to 1914, Norway saw a period of great economic growth. By 1914, Norway had the fourth-largest

Below: Founded in 1050, Norway's capital city of Oslo became a thriving economic center in the early twentieth century.

merchant fleet in the world. When World War I began that year, however, the Germans destroyed half of the fleet, even though Norway had declared itself **neutral**. During World War II, Germany again attacked Norway, although the country was again neutral. The **Nazi** government occupied Norway until 1945 but faced strong **resistance** from the Norwegians. When the war ended, 10,262 Norwegians had been killed, and many cities were destroyed.

Above: Although Norway took a neutral stand during World War I, the country's merchant fleet carried oil and supplies to Allied Forces around the world.

Modern Times

In 1945, Norway became a founding member of the United Nations. Norway also belongs to the North Atlantic Treaty Organization (NATO) and the Organization for Security and Cooperation in Europe (OSCE). In 1952, Norway became part of the Nordic Council, along with Denmark, Finland, Iceland, and Sweden. In 1994, the people of Norway voted against joining the European Union.

Below: Norway joined NATO in 1949 when it realized it could no longer be neutral in times of war. NATO is an alliance of nineteen countries from North America and Europe. Its fiftieth anniversary was celebrated in Washington, D.C., in 1999.

Olaf II Haraldsson (c. 995–1030)

The country's first king, Olaf II Haraldsson, is also called Saint Olaf. The **patron saint** of Norway, Olaf II was made a saint in 1164 because of the miracles that were said to have happened when he died in battle.

Fridtjof Nansen (1861–1930)

One of the great explorers from **Scandinavia**, Fridtjof Nansen visited Greenland and wrote three books about his explorations. Nansen was awarded the Nobel Peace Prize in 1922 for his work with the Red Cross during the Russian **famine**.

Fridtjof Nansen

Gro Harlem Brundtland (1939–)

Appointed Norway's first female prime minister in 1981, Dr. Gro Harlem Brundtland made great contributions to children's health and disease prevention. In 1998, she became Director-General of the World Health Organization (WHO).

Gro Harlem Brundtland

15

Government and the Economy

Norway is a constitutional monarchy. The king is the head of state. Power is held by the Council of State, which includes an elected Prime Minister and ministers appointed by the king.

Laws are passed by the *Storting* (STOOR-teeng), a legislative body with 165 members who hold four-year terms. The king, however, can reject bills or actions the group recommends.

Below: The Storting consists of two houses. The *Lagting* (LOG-teeng), or upper house, is the smaller of the two. The *Odelsting* (OO-dels-teeng), or lower house, is much larger with 75 percent of the members.

Eight members of the Storting are directly elected by the people. The other members are nominated by their political parties and elected by their respective counties. In the 1990s, women made up more than one-third of the Storting.

The king appoints judges who are nominated by the Ministry of Justice. A Chief Justice heads the Supreme Court.

Above: Norway has twenty-four political parties that can nominate candidates for election to the Storting. Since 1965, Norway has been ruled by governments made up of many parties because no single party has been successful in capturing a majority of the votes.

Economy

In the 1960s, oil was discovered in the North Sea. Since then, oil has become an important part of the economy. Norway is the world's third-largest petroleum exporter. The country's many rivers, waterfalls, and glaciers have enabled it to become Europe's largest provider of hydroelectric power.

Agriculture, Forestry, and Fishing

Farming makes up only 2 percent of the economy in Norway. Forests cover one-fifth of the land. The third-largest export industry is the forest industry.

Fishing is an important part of the economy, but the number of people who work in the industry is dropping.

Exports and Imports

Norway's main trading partners are Germany, Sweden, and the United Kingdom. Norway exports machinery, fish, metals, metal products, and petroleum. It imports heavy machinery, equipment, food, and other goods.

Below: Forests in Norway are mostly in the eastern and central parts of the country. This timber mill is in Telemark.

People and Lifestyle

Most Norwegians have blond hair, blue eyes, and the same ethnic origins. The largest **minority group** in Norway is the Sami. The Sami were Norway's first inhabitants. The Sami Parliament has represented them in politics since 1989. Today, nearly twenty thousand Sami live in Norway.

Finnish-speaking people make up another minority group. Finns began to migrate to Norway in the eighteenth century. Some came to find a better life, others to escape war and famine.

Left: People in Norway live long, healthy lives. The life expectancy is seventy-six years for men and eighty-two years for women. More than three-quarters of Norwegians live in urban areas.

Other Minority Groups

Besides the Sami and the Finns, other minority groups living in Norway are the Ethiopians, the Pakistanis, the Iranians, the Swedes, and the Danes. These groups comprise about 6 percent of the population. The government conducts free Norwegian language lessons for all new citizens to help them fit into society.

Above: The Sami traditionally herd reindeer and wear brightly colored costumes. Over the years, some Sami have converted from their traditional beliefs to become Christians. This Sami family gathers for an Easter meal.

Family Life

Norway is ranked by the United Nations as having the highest standard of living in the world. Families in Norway are usually small, often with just two children. In many families, both parents work, but family relationships are still important.

People in Norway pay high taxes to help fund the **welfare** system, which includes programs that provide for the needs of families and children.

Above: The woman at the far left is wearing the traditional costume of Norway, known as the *bunad*. A man's bunad includes a jacket, vest, cap, dark breeches, and socks. In the past, most Norwegians wore the bunad every day. Today, it is worn only on special occasions. Most people prefer to wear Western-style clothes.

City Living

Norwegian cities are very clean and green. Many parks are found within cities, and wilderness areas are close.

Rural Living

Because Norway is mountainous, some areas are **isolated** from each other. The distances between people have caused many different communities and **dialects** to develop. The government provides funds to improve the quality of life in these areas. It also conducts training programs for rural youths.

Above: Some of the people living in the Norwegian countryside still lead a traditional way of life and farm for a living.

Below: With a population of over five hundred thousand people, Norway's busiest city is Oslo.

Education

All children in Norway must complete ten years of basic education in three stages: lower primary, upper primary, and lower secondary. They study subjects such as religion, Norwegian, and English. They can also study a third language. After lower secondary school, students may go on to upper secondary school. They can choose either general or vocational studies.

Left: Norway has one of the highest literacy rates in the world, and most Norwegians can read and write. To encourage learning, schoolwork is not graded for primary school students. Students only start to receive grades when they go to secondary school.

General studies prepare students for higher learning at a university. Vocational studies help them learn skills that enable them to work.

Admission to a university is based on performance in upper secondary school. Of the four universities in Norway, the oldest is the University of Oslo, which was founded in 1811. Norwegian students also have other choices for higher learning, including six private colleges, twenty-six state colleges, and two art colleges.

Above: These Sami children, dressed in their traditional costumes, attend special schools with programs teaching their culture and traditions. A center for Sami Studies at the University of Tromsø also caters to people who want to know more about the people and their culture.

Religion

The official church of Norway is the Evangelical Lutheran Church. About 86 percent of the people are members. In school, children learn about religion, including the beliefs of other religions. The subject is taught through songs, stories, and discussions. Norway allows its people freedom of religion. Other religious groups include Methodists, Baptists, Free Lutherans, Muslims, Pentecostals, and Roman Catholics.

Above: Sami people attend a Lutheran church service in Finnmark. Both men and women can serve as officials in the Evangelical Lutheran church. The country's first female pastor was appointed in 1961, and the first female bishop was appointed in 1993.

Ancient Norse Gods

In ancient times, Norwegian people worshipped Norse Gods. Although this practice is no longer continued today, Norse gods live on in traditional stories and poetry, which are full of their exciting adventures. Famous Norse gods include Odin, god of war and wisdom; Thor, god of thunder and storms; Frey, god of fertility and peace; Tyr, the bravest warrior; and Freya, Earth goddess and patron of pleasure.

Below: Norway has many statues and illustrations that depict different Norse gods. Odin (*left*) is the god of war and wisdom. Freya (*right*) is the goddess of pleasure.

Language

The two official forms of Norwegian are New Norwegian, or *Nynorsk* (NEE-nohrsk), and Dano-Norwegian, or *Bokmål* (BOOK-mohl). Bokmål is the more popular of the two. Most books and magazines are written in Bokmål. Many Norwegians wanted their own unique language, which led to the creation of *Samnorsk* (SAWM-nohrsk) recently. Most of the Sami people speak their own dialects.

Left: Norwegian teenagers look at movie posters. Three extra letters — æ, ø, and å — are used in the Norwegian alphabet.

Literature

One of Norway's Nobel prize winners for literature was Bjørnstjerne Bjørnson (1893–1910). His poem, "Ja, vi elsker dette landet," was adopted as the national anthem. Another Nobel prize winner for literature was Sigrid Undset (1882–1949) in 1928. The most famous Norwegian writer is playwright Henrik Ibsen (1828–1906). He is known as the "Father of Modern Drama."

Sagas are historical tales about Viking history, adventures, and travels. Children often hear them from parents.

Arts

Architecture

Wood is often used as a building material for Norwegian homes because it is so plentiful. In the past, wealthy people built their homes of stone. Wooden houses, however, are naturally warmer. Samis in the north of Norway use **turf**, which keeps their homes warm during the long, cold winters.

Below: Parts of the Nidaros Cathedral were restored in 1897 by Gustav Vigeland, the most famous sculptor in Norway.

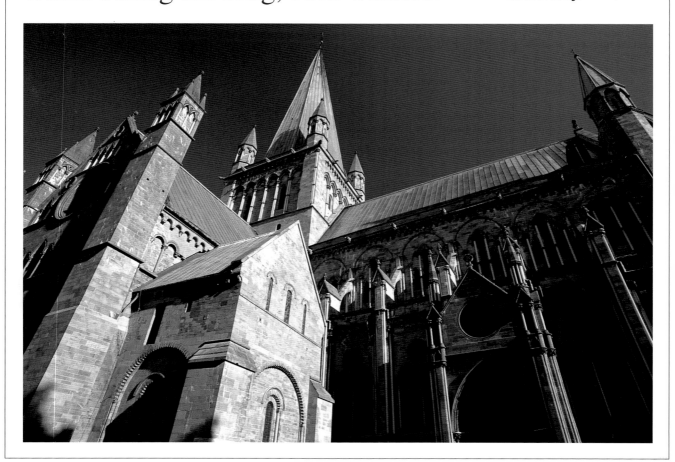

Left: Norway's famous stave churches are made of wood. Stave churches have high roofs with detailed paintings on the walls inside. Traditional Viking carvings decorate many of the door frames, walls, and staves.

Stave Churches

The Vikings started building wooden churches about a thousand years ago. The wooden support posts are called staves, so the churches are known as stave churches.

A Center for the Arts

Oslo's National Gallery is the largest art museum in the country. The Oslo Philharmonic is the main orchestra of Norway. Oslo is also home to the Norwegian Film Institute and the Norwegian Folk Museum.

Painters

Norway's best-known painter is Edvard Munch (1863–1944). His most famous painting is *The Scream,* which he painted in 1893. Other popular painters are Axel Revold (1887–1962) and Alf Rolfsen (1895–1979).

Delicate Rosemaling

Rosemaling (ROO-seh-mohling), or "rose painting," is a traditional style of painting dating from the 1600s. Flower patterns in curls and twists are painted on bowls, plates, and other items.

Above: Visitors admire a painting in Norway's largest art gallery, the National Gallery in Oslo.

A Rich Musical Legacy

The famous Norwegian composer Edvard Grieg (1843–1870) was influenced by Norwegian folk songs. He composed music for the play *Peer Gynt*. Violinist Ole Bornemann Bull (1810–1880) was another famous musician. The Hardanger fiddle is a traditional Norwegian musical instrument. It looks like an ordinary violin, but it produces a unique sound with an extra set of strings.

Above: Edvard Grieg is one of Norway's best-known composers.

Below: A musician shows off his Hardanger fiddle.

Leisure

Allemannsretten (AWL-leh-mawns-reht-ten) means "Every Man's Right." A Norwegian law by that name allows people to go anywhere in the country, including the many forests. Some wilderness areas are not far from cities. Many people own cabins in remote places and reach them by hiking. Some of the cabins have no electricity, so people must use lanterns and candles.

Below: Boating is a popular activity in the summer.

Norwegians enjoy skiing in winter. School children hike on nature trails and learn how to camp in snow.

During summer, Norwegians swim, fish, and sail in the country's many fjords, lakes, and rivers. They also enjoy hiking in the mountains and searching for wild berries to make into traditional jams and desserts.

Norwegians love to spend time with their friends. They often visit each other at home because eating at restaurants can be expensive.

Above: Norwegians love the outdoors, and adults often organize simple but fun games, such as tug-of-war, for the children.

Exhilarating Winter Sports

Norwegians love skiing, both alpine, or downhill, and cross-country. Ski jumping is another popular sport. Skiers race down long, narrow slopes and jump off as far as they can. One of the most difficult ski jumps in the world, the Holmenkollen Ski Jump, is in Norway. Norwegians are also good at speed skating. Johann Olav Koss won three gold medals for the sport at the 1994 Winter Olympic Games held in Lillehammer, Norway.

Above: Norway is the birthplace of skiing. In 1862, the country held the world's first ski jumping contest.

Summer Sports

The most popular sport in Norway is soccer, or *fotball* (FOOT-bawl). The women's national soccer team won medals at the 1996 and 2000 Olympic Games and at the 1995 World Cup. The men's national team placed third at the 1936 Olympic Games. The team qualified for the World Cup in 1938, 1994, and 1998. In addition to soccer, children in Norway enjoy handball, skiing, and swimming.

Below: Norway's location beside the sea enables people who love the outdoors to compete in sailboat races.

Holidays and Festivals

Norwegians take a vacation during Easter week. Many people camp, hike, stay in a cabin, or go skiing. Some go to church on Easter Sunday.

On June 23, Norwegians observe *Sankthansaften* (SAWNKT-hawns-awf-tehn), or Midsummer's Eve.

The Norwegian **constitution** was signed on May 17, 1814. The nation celebrates its independence each year on that date. Many towns have games, contests, food, music, and parades.

Above: People in Norway light **bonfires** on Midsummer's Eve. In the past, the fires were lit to protect them from evil spirits. Now the fires are meeting places for friends and relatives.

Left: During the Midsummer's Eve celebration, boys and girls in Norway dress in traditional clothes.

Left: Christmas trees in Norway are sometimes decorated with small Norwegian flags. Presents are placed below the Christmas tree.

Christmas

Norwegians call Christmas *Jul* (YOOL). A tradition called *ringe julen* (REEN-geh YOOL-ehn) means "ringing in Christmas." Church bells ring at five o'clock on Christmas Eve to signal the start of Christmas. People celebrate on Christmas Eve with a traditional dinner. Then they exchange gifts. They may also attend church.

Food

Norwegians eat four meals a day. At *frokost* (FROOK-oost), or breakfast, they may eat porridge or other cereals and open-faced sandwiches. *Lunsj* (LOON-sh), or lunch, may be a large snack. Sometimes people eat a snack between breakfast and lunch, too. The only hot meal of the day is dinner, or *middag* (MIH-dawg). Some people also eat a later meal called *kveldsmat* (keh-VELL-dis-mawt) with tea or coffee.

Above: Cod is hung to dry on wooden posts. It can be eaten dried or boiled and softened. Dried cod is a popular food in Norway.

Left: Dinner is eaten in the early evening. It often includes soup, bread, and a main course of seafood.

Bread is a main part of the Norwegian diet. People in Norway often eat open-faced sandwiches. They eat bread with salted herring, brown goat cheese, cold meats, and spreads made of vegetables, shrimp, or sweets. *Flatbrød* (FLAWT-brohd) is a kind of thin, crisp bread. It is often eaten with stews.

Gomme (GOO-meh) is a popular sweet milk dish that people eat with waffles. A sour cream porridge called *rømmegrøt* (ROHM-meh-groht) is often served at weddings.

41

A | B | C | D

1

NORWEGIAN SEA

SVALBARD

Tromsø

1 Finnmark

2 Troms

N

2

Arctic Circle

Arctic Circle

Province
Boundary

International
Boundary

Capital

City

River

3 Nordland

FINLAND

NORTH
ATLANTIC
OCEAN

3

SWEDEN

4 Nord-Trøndelag

Trondheim

5

6

Galdhöpiggen
(8,100 ft / 2,469 m)
Jostedalsbreen

9

Sogne Fjord

4

8

7

10

11

12

Haugesund

15

18

17

16

14

13

19 OSLO

5

NORTH SEA

NORWAY

1 Finnmark
2 Troms
3 Nordland
4 Nord-Trøndelag
5 Sør-Trøndelag
6 More og Romsdal
7 Hedmark
8 Oppland
9 Sogn og Fjordane
10 Hordaland
11 Buskerud
12 Akershus
13 Østfold
14 Vestfold
15 Telemark
16 Aust-Agder
17 Vest-Agder
18 Rogaland
19 Oslo

42

Above: Many towns in Norway are located very close to the sea.

Akershus (county) B4–B5
Aust-Agder (county) A5–B5

Buskerud (county) A4–B5

Finland C1–D5
Finnmark (county) A1–D2

Galdhöpiggen A4
Glåma (river) B4–B5

Hedmark (county) B4–B5
Hordaland (county) A4–A5

Jostedalsbreen (glacier) A4

Lagen (river) A4–B4

More og Romsdal (county) A3–B4

Nordland (county) B2–C3
Nord-Norge (region) B3–D1
Nord-Trøndelag (county) B3
North Atlantic Ocean A4–B3
North Sea A5–B5
Norwegian Sea B2–C1

Oppland (county) A4–B5
Oslo B5
Østfold (county) B5
Østlandet (region) A5–B4

Rogaland (county) A5
Russia D1–D2

Sogne Fjord A4
Sogn og Fjordane (county) A4
Sørlandet (region) B4–B5
Sør-Trøndelag (county) B3–B4
Svalbard A1–A2
Sweden B5–D2

Telemark (county) A4–B5

Troms (county) C2–D1
Tromsø C1
Trøndelag (region) B3–B4
Trøndheim B3

Vest-Agder (county) A5
Vestfold (county) B5
Vestlandet (region) A5–B3

Quick Facts

Official Name   Kingdom of Norway

Capital   Oslo

Official Language   Norwegian

Population   4,525,116 (2003 estimate)

Land Area   118,834 square miles (307,860 square km)

Regions   Nord-Norge, Østlandet, Sørlandet, Trøndelag, Vestlandet

Counties   Akershus, Aust-Agder, Buskerud, Finnmark, Hedmark, Hordaland, More og Romsdal, Nordland, Nord-Trøndelag, Oppland, Oslo, Østfold, Rogaland, Sogn og Fjordane, Sør-Trøndelag, Telemark, Troms, Vest-Agder, Vestfold

Highest Point   Galdhöpiggen 8,100 feet (2,469 m)

Major Rivers   Glåma, Lagen

Main Religion   Evangelical Lutheranism

Major Holidays   Easter week (March/April), Constitution Day (May 17), Midsummer's Eve (June 23), Christmas (December 24)

Currency   Krone (NOK 7.3 = U.S. $1 in 2003)

Opposite: The main street in Oslo is Karl Johans Gate, which connects the central railroad to the Royal Palace.

Glossary

aggressive: strong and forceful; ready to attack.

bonfires: large fires built in the open for warmth or entertainment or as a signal.

constitution: a set of laws that establish how a country is governed and the rights of its people.

descendant: a person whose birth can be traced back to a specific ancestor.

dialects: varieties of a language that are spoken in different parts of a country.

domesticated: tamed.

famine: a great lack of food.

fjords: narrow inlets of the sea between steep slopes or cliffs.

glaciers: large bodies of ice that move slowly down mountains or spread across land.

Gulf Stream: a warm ocean current.

hydroelectric power: electricity that is produced when water passes through a dam and into a river below.

inhabitants: people who live in a particular place.

isolated: separated from others.

merchant fleet: a country's ships used for trade or commerce.

minority group: a group of people who are different from the rest of the population in terms of race, religion, or ethnic background.

Nazi: the political party of Adolf Hitler. It controlled Germany from 1933 to 1945.

neutral: not taking sides in a war or an argument.

patron saint: a saint who is believed to protect a particular place or group of people.

plague: an infectious disease that spreads quickly and causes a large number of deaths.

resistance: an opposing force

Scandinavia: group name for the countries of Norway, Denmark, Sweden, Finland, and Iceland.

trolls: imaginary beings with special powers that are said to live in hills and caves.

turf: a layer of earth and grass.

welfare: money or other aid given by the government to people in need.

More Books to Read

Christmas in Norway. Christmas Around the World series. Kristin Thoennes (Bridgestone Books)

Favorite Fairy Tales Told in Norway. Favorite Fairy Tales series. Virginia Haviland (Beech Tree Books)

Norway. Countries of the World series. Kathleen Deady (Bridgestone Books)

Norway. Ticket to series. Deborah L. Kopka (Carolrhoda)

Norway. True Books – Geography: Countries series. Elaine Landau (Children's Book Press)

Norway in Pictures. Visual Geography series. Eric Braun (Lerner Publications)

The Race of the Birkbeiners. Lise Lunge-Larsen (Houghton Mifflin Company)

Roald Amundsen. Great Explorers series. Enid Broderick (World Almanac Education)

The Troll with No Heart in His Body. Lise Lunge-Larsen (Houghton Mifflin Company)

Who's That Knocking on Christmas Eve? Jan Brett (Putnam Publishing)

Videos

Around Stavanger Norway. (Jan Kurtis Skugstad)

Norway. (Lonely Planet)

Rogaland the Jewel of Norway (Jan Kurtis Skugstad)

Scandinavia: Denmark, Sweden and Norway (Questar)

Websites

www.jorgetutor.com/noruega/noruega.htm

www.kongehuset.no

www.lysator.liu.se/nordic/scn/faq23.html

www.sofn.com:8080/index.jsp

Due to the dynamic nature of the Internet, some web sites stay current longer than others. To find additional web sites, use a reliable search engine with one or more of the following keywords to help you locate information about Norway. Keywords: *fjords, Henrik Ibsen, Olaf II Haraldsson, Oslo, rosemaling, Sami, Vikings.*

Index